THE LOCKERBIE
AIRLINE CRASH

by
Madelyn Horton

LUCENT
B·O·O·K·S

WORLD DISASTERS

These and other titles are available in the Lucent World Disasters Series:

The Armenian Earthquake	The Exxon-Valdez Oil Spill
The Bhopal Chemical Leak	The Hindenburg
The Black Death	Hiroshima
The Challenger	The Irish Potato Famine
Chernobyl	Krakatoa
The Chicago Fire	The Lockerbie Airline Crash
The Children's Crusade	Pompeii
The Crash of 1929	The San Francisco Earthquake
The Dust Bowl	Smallpox and the American Indian
The Ethiopian Famine	The Titanic

Library of Congress Cataloging-in-Publication Data

Madelyn Horton, 1962-
  The Lockerbie airline crash / by Madelyn Horton.
    p.   cm. — (World disasters)
  Includes bibliographical references and index.
  Summary: Examines the terrorist incident which caused the explosion and crash of a Pan Am 747 over the Scottish village of Lockerbie in 1988.
  ISBN 1-56006-017-4 (lib. : acid-free paper)
  1. Pan Am Flight 103 Bombing Incident, 1988—Juvenile literature. 2. Terrorism—United States—Juvenile literature. 3. Terrorism—Europe—Juvenile literature. 4. Victims of terrorism—Scotland—Lockerbie—Juvenile literature. [1. Pan Am Flight 103 Bombing Incident, 1988. 2. Terrorism. 3. Aeronautics—Accidents.]
  I. Title. II. Series.
HV6431.H67 1991
363.12'465'0941483—dc20   91-25741

To Christopher and Nicholas

Table of Contents

Preface
The World Disasters Series

World disasters have always aroused human curiosity. Whenever news of tragedy spreads, we want to learn more about it. We wonder how and why the disaster happened, how people reacted, and whether we might have acted differently. To be sure, disaster evokes a wide range of responses—fear, sorrow, despair, generosity, even hope. Yet from every great disaster, one remarkable truth always seems to emerge: in spite of death, pain, and destruction, the human spirit triumphs.

History is full of disasters, arising from a variety of causes. Earthquakes, floods, volcanic eruptions, and other natural events often produce widespread destruction. Just as often, however, people accidentally bring suffering and distress on themselves and other human beings. And many disasters have sinister causes, like human greed, envy, or prejudice.

The disasters included in this series have been chosen not only for their dramatic qualities, but also for their educational value. The reader will learn about the causes and effects of the greatest disasters in history. Technical concepts and interesting anecdotes are explained and illustrated in inset boxes.

But disasters should not be viewed in isolation. To enrich the reader's understanding, these books present historical information about the time period, and interesting facts about the culture in which each disaster occurred. Finally, they teach valuable lessons about human nature. More acts of bravery, cowardice, intelligence, and foolishness are compressed into the few days of a disaster than most people experience in a lifetime.

Dramatic illustrations and evocative narrative lure the reader to distant cities and times gone by. Readers witness the awesome power of an exploding volcano, the magnitude of a violent earthquake, and the hopelessness of passengers on a mighty ship passing to its watery grave. By reliving the events, the reader will see how disaster affects the lives of real people and will gain a deeper understanding of their sorrow, their pain, their courage, and their hope.

Introduction

Terrorist Attack

On the rainy afternoon of December 21, 1988, Pan Am Flight 103 took off from Heathrow Airport on its regularly scheduled flight from London to New York. The plane was to stop at New York's JFK Airport then continue on to Detroit, its final destination. Among the passengers were U.S. military personnel, college students from an overseas studies program, and excited Christmas travelers. The overhead compartments were stuffed with gaily wrapped presents in anticipation of the upcoming holidays.

The flight was to be anything but routine, though. Just over a half an hour after take-off, as the plane was flying over the village of Lockerbie, Scotland, a bomb exploded deep in a cargo hold, causing the jumbo jet to rip apart in mid-air, 31,000 feet above the earth. All 259 people aboard the plane were killed in the fiery explosion. The burning wreckage and debris that fell from the sky killed eleven more people on the ground at Lockerbie.

The disaster was among the worst in aviation history. A full-scale investigation was launched immediately. What had caused the explosion? Was it structural failure? Engine trouble? Or was the plane deliberately destroyed by a bomb that was somehow smuggled on board? If it was a bomb, how did it get past airport security? Who was behind the bombing, and why?

The Case Is Not Closed

Since the tragic events of that December day, the Lockerbie investigators have learned a great deal about the circumstances surrounding Flight 103. What they have uncovered along the way is as disturbing as the disaster itself. But the case is not closed yet. A handful of important questions remain unsolved. Answering these questions remains a crucial task if future crashes like the one at Lockerbie are to be avoided.

The Lockerbie Air Crash in History

2350 BC
Sumerian civilization begins in Mesopotamia (present-day Iraq)

330 BC
Alexander the Great conquers the Middle East

1500 AD
Leonardo da Vinci draws plans for a flying machine

1783
Frenchmen Joseph and Jacques Montgolfier invent the hot-air balloon

1903
Wright brothers make first successful airplane flight

1914
World War I begins; first use of airplanes in war

1927
Charles Lindbergh makes first solo transatlantic flight

1939
World War II begins; 6 million Jews die in Nazi holocaust

1945
U.S. B-29 bomber drops atomic bomb on Hiroshima, Japan

1947
Against Arab opposition, United Nations votes to create independent state of Israel in Palestine

1956
Israelis successfully defeat Egypt for control of Suez Canal but withdraw from Suez after pressure from United Nations

1964
Palestine Liberation Organization (PLO) established. Its stated goal is to free Palestine of Israeli presence using violence and terrorism

1966
Soviet-supported Syria begins terrorist attacks on Israel

1967
Six Day War: Egyptian forces invade Israeli-held Sinai Peninsula; Israeli jets wipe out Egyptian, Syrian, and Jordanian air bases; Israel defeats Arabs in six days; seizes territory that quadruples its size

1972
Arab terrorists take eleven Israeli athletes hostage at Olympics in Munich, Germany, and demand the release of Israeli-held Arab prisoners; when Israel refuses to comply, terrorists murder the hostages

1973
Egypt and Syria attack Israel by surprise on Jewish Holiday of Yom Kippur; Israelis suffer heavy losses but regain territory taken by the Arab forces

1976
Israeli commandoes rescue passengers of airliner hijacked by PLO terrorists at Entebbe, Uganda

1978
Israel invades Lebanon to destroy PLO bases after a PLO terrorist raid kills 30 civilians in Israel

1981
Israeli jet fighters destroy an Iraqi nuclear power plant. Israel claims plant was building nuclear weapons to use against Israel

1985
Explosion aboard Air India flight off the coast of Ireland kills 329. In first Western retaliation to terrorism, U.S. commandoes capture terrorists who hijacked Italian cruise ship *Achille Lauro* as they attempt to escape from Egypt.

1986
U.S. fighter jets attack alleged terrorist-run chemical weapons plant in Libya

1987
Palestinians in Israel's West Bank riot to protest Israeli mistreatment; riot unifies Palestinians who declare West Bank and Gaza Strip an independent Palestinian state in 1988. 115 die in Korean Air jetliner mid-air explosion

1988
July: USS *Vincennes* mistakes Iranian civilian airliner for a military bomber, destroys it, killing all 290 passengers. December: terrorist bomb explodes aboard Pan-Am Flight 103 over Lockerbie, Scotland, killing all 259 passengers and 11 people on the ground.

1989
Mid-air explosion of French airliner over Niger, Africa kills 171. Bomb under seat aboard Colombian Avianca flight explodes near Bogota, killing 107

1990
Iraq invades and annexes Kuwait; in response, UN Allied forces amass in Saudi Arabia; set January 15, 1991 deadline for Iraqi withdrawal

1991
U.S.-led air attacks by Allied forces liberate Kuwait, destroy Iraqi forces. Israel vows future retaliation for Iraqi missile attacks on Tel Aviv

One

An Unlikely Spot for Disaster

Lockerbie is a tiny village tucked into the fertile Annandale Valley of southern Scotland, where winters are damp and drizzly and the summers are cool and mild. The surrounding country stretches into rich green farmland and gently rolling hills. Scottish blackface sheep, whose wool is used to produce the tweeds for which Scotland is famous, roam the hillsides. Among the writers who have called southern Scotland home are novelist Sir Walter Scott and historian Thomas Carlyle.

An ancient place, Lockerbie still holds annual sheep sales as it has since 1680. In those days the town had been a busier, less peaceful, place. During the last half of the sixteenth century, the Scottish warred with the British over border terri-tory, and thousands of lives were lost in the fighting at Lockerbie. In the century before that, hundreds died in clan wars between the Johnstone family, who occupied the middle of the valley, and the Maxwell family, who held the lower end. But Lockerbie's history goes back even further: in a local quarry, fossil hunters have uncovered the footprints of dino-saurs.

In the late 1980s, though, Lockerbie was simply a peaceful farming village of 3,000 people. The people who lived in Lockerbie lived quietly, their ways untouched by the bustle of city life.

Christmas in Lockerbie

Just before seven o'clock on a damp December night in Locker-bie, Ella Ramsden sat down to read the day's delivery of Christmas cards. Her son Jimmy and his wife and the two boys, Ramsden's grand-children, had left at noon that day to return to their home in West Ger-many. They had celebrated Christ-mas early and Ramsden had rel-ished every minute. It was the first family reunion in more than three years. Alone now, she felt a little sad. She settled herself before the fire.

Across town, fourteen-year-old Stephen Flannigan had finished having tea with his mother and sis-ter and left his home in the Sher-wood Crescent housing estate to go to a neighbor's house. His friend, David Edwards, was good with bikes, and Stephen had brought along his sister's bike, which had a flat tire. The two boys were in the garage ex-

The ancient town of Lockerbie, Scotland. Lockerbie is a rural town and many of its residents farm for a living.

amining the damage.

At his farmhouse three miles outside of town, Jimmie Wilson relaxed in the kitchen with his wife June and their daughter Lesley, enjoying an after-dinner cup of coffee. Their decorated Christmas tree stood near the dining-room window, where its bright lights cast holiday cheer into the winter night.

It was December 21, just four days before Christmas, and a few people hurried from shop to shop along the streets of Lockerbie. Colorful lights twinkled in store windows.

Meanwhile, in London, Pan Am Flight 103 had just lifted off the ground, twenty-five minutes past its scheduled 6:00 P.M. departure time. On the second leg of a long journey, the flight had begun earlier in the day at Frankfurt, West Germany, on a Boeing 727. At Heathrow Airport, passengers and baggage from the 727 were transferred to the bigger Boeing 747 for the trip overseas. A number of new passengers also boarded the plane at Heathrow. Flight 103 would stop at JFK Airport in New York, then continue on to its final destination, Detroit Metropolitan Airport.

The Passengers and Crew

On board were 259 people, including a sixteen-member flight crew. The pilot, fifty-five-year-old Captain Jim MacQuarrie, was an experienced airman. On land, the father of two enjoyed working on his two-hundred-year-old colonial home in New Hampshire. MacQuarrie's co-pilot, Ray Wagner, also

had two children; his daughters were Olympic-class swimmers, and he himself liked to coach swimming. The flight attendants on board Flight 103 represented many countries, including Sweden, Spain, and the Philippines. Among them were three Americans. The youngest, twenty-year-old Stacie Franklin of San Diego, California, had just started her job with Pan Am.

The passengers settled in for the seven hour flight. They, too, were a diverse lot, including university students, business people, and military personnel from U.S. bases in West Germany. Most were headed home for the holidays, and the overhead compartments bulged with handsomely wrapped presents. Festivity and anticipation charged the air.

Thirty-five students from Syracuse University in New York were returning home that evening, having completed a fast-paced overseas study program in London. Twenty-year-old Theodora Cohen, traveling to her parents' Long Island house, had spent an exciting semester studying drama. Another student, twenty-one-year-old Mark Tobin, had spent time at the respected British Broadcasting Company (BBC). He hoped to use the experience to achieve a career as a sports broadcaster. Karen Hunt, a junior year English major, had enjoyed her semester abroad, but she had missed her family, too, and would be happy to arrive home.

Many of Flight 103's business passengers had wrapped up meetings and projects in time to travel for the holidays. Diane Maslowski, a stockbroker for a big London firm, was keeping her yearly tradition of returning to her parents' New Jersey home for Christmas. David Trimmer-Smith, newly married and a vice-president of Oxford University Press in the United States, had been to a sales conference in Oxford. Two senior executives of Volkswagen of America, James Fuller and Lou Marengo, were returning home from three days of business meetings in West Germany. Fuller's work took him to West Germany often, and he had flown Flight 103 before. So, probably, had the many U.S. military personnel stationed at West German bases who were flying to the States to join families for the holidays.

A successful mission was bringing Michael Bernstein home. A lawyer for the U.S. Department of Justice

---

FLIGHT 103 BACKGROUND

Pan Am Flight 103, also known as the *Maid of the Seas*, was a 747, the fifteenth to be built by Boeing and, in 1988, one of the oldest jumbo jets flying. Since February 1970, the *Maid of the Seas* had flown seventy-two thousand hours and taken off and landed 16,500 times. Even so, it was well below the number of takeoff and landing cycles considered high, which is 50,000.

The 747 is the largest commercial aircraft built, capable of carrying four hundred passengers. It is so big that one wing alone weighs twenty-eight thousand pounds, and its wing area is larger than three three-bedroom houses combined. Its tail is equal to the height of a six-story building.

All the safety features common to modern airplanes were present on the *Maid of the Seas*. The plane also had the all-important black box, the first thing investigators search for if a crash occurs. The box contains a recorder that captures all the flight data, such as altitude and air speed, and all conversation between the pilot and air-traffic controllers. If there is a crash, investigators try to determine what went wrong by listening to what was recorded on the black box.

The Boeing 747, the largest commercial aircraft ever built.

Office of Special Investigations, Bernstein's job was to track down Nazi war criminals living in the United States and ensure they faced prosecution. He had been in Austria, attempting to negotiate the deportation of a former Nazi guard at Auschwitz. The guard had entered the United States in 1952 by giving false information. After three days, Bernstein had finally convinced the Austrian authorities to accept the man into their country. Bernstein

felt tired, but satisfied, as he boarded Flight 103. He was anxious to see his wife, Stephanie, and his two children, seven-year-old Sarah and four-year-old Joseph.

Ingrid Smith was going to meet her husband in the United States. She had flown many times in the four years that she had been married to Bruce, a pilot for Pan Am. His generous travel benefits had allowed her to see Europe and South America. Now she would join him

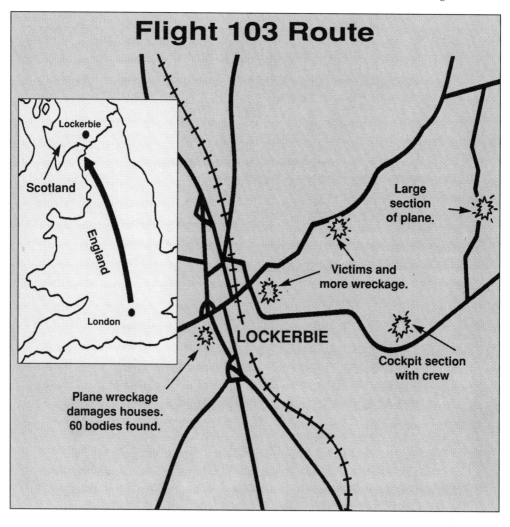

Flight 103 Route

Lockerbie

Scotland

England

London

LOCKERBIE

Large section of plane.

Victims and more wreckage.

Cockpit section with crew

Plane wreckage damages houses. 60 bodies found.

Pilot James MacQuarrie   Passenger Karen Hunt   Passenger Lou Marengo

As passengers boarded Flight 103, they had no idea that the flight would be anything but routine.

in New York to spend the holidays with him and his two children. At the moment, Bruce was flying, too, piloting a jet from Bermuda to New York.

Twenty-nine-year-old Garima Rattan had just been to New Delhi with her husband and two small children to attend a family wedding. There she had proudly shown three-year-old Suruchi and two-year-old Anmol to all the relatives, many of whom had never met the children. The celebration had been wonderful. The trip home to Michigan was going to be long, though. They had boarded the plane in Frankfurt, and once they reached New York they would still have to fly to Detroit. Her husband had returned the day before, and she was eager to reunite the family.

While the flight attendants served drinks and handed out headphones for the in-flight movie, far below

Ella Ramsden opened Christmas mail and the Wilsons poured another cup of coffee. Stephen Flannigan had almost finished patching his sister's tire. In the tranquil town of Lockerbie, people went about their normal business.

As the jumbo jet climbed higher into the sky, reunion undoubtedly filled the thoughts of Flight 103's passengers. The weather was favorable for flying: rain falling at Heathrow was nothing more than a drizzle, and the stiff winds would hardly bother an aircraft the size of a 747. Some of the passengers had uneventfully flown this route before. Nothing indicated that this flight might be anything but normal.

At least, not anything that the passengers could see. But if they had known what airline security expert Isaac Yeffet and a handful of others knew, they might have thought differently.

Two

Terrorism Contributes to Disaster

Terrorists want to change social, economic, or political conditions but lack the power to do so. Unable to use conventional means, in desperation they turn to violence. They believe that destroying buildings, airplanes, or people will draw attention to their cause and help bring about change. They expect people to agree to their demands out of fear of future attacks.

In carrying out their acts of violence, terrorists tend to choose places where people gather—bus stations, train depots, shopping districts. The public places that seem most susceptible to terrorist attack, however, are airports and airplanes, where crowds are usually large and the potential for damage is great.

Terrorists aim for high visibility. They know that the greater the damage, the more people will notice.

Throughout the 1970s heavily armed terrorists often carried out hijackings. Holding an airplane full of passengers hostage, and sometimes injuring or killing them, hijackers would demand that the pilot fly to the destination they named. To counteract hijackings, airlines had to create strict security measures. The X-ray machine, in particular, helped to screen luggage or passengers for hidden weapons.

The late 1980s signaled a sudden need for greater vigilance, as terrorists developed dangerous new tactics and increased their attacks. On April 2, 1986, in Athens, Greece, a bomb exploded aboard TWA Flight 840 as the plane waited on the ground. It killed four people, including a four-month-old baby. The incident made one point frighteningly clear: As it became more difficult for terrorists to smuggle guns aboard planes, they increasingly turned to more sophisticated methods. They had moved into high-technology weapons and were designing bombs that could escape detection by airport X-ray machines.

A Specially Designed Bomb

The bomb that exploded on TWA Flight 840 was specially designed to be triggered by barometric pressure: It would go off only when the plane had reached a preset altitude. In this way, bombs could do the most damage with the fewest traces of evidence. Made with a thin layer of

Terrorists are usually politically motivated. Throughout the 1970s and through today, terrorist acts occur. Here, terrorists hijack a TWA Airliner in Beirut Airport in 1985.

AIRPORT SECURITY

With the rise of hijacking attempts in the late 1960s and early 1970s, airport security became a necessity. The ability to detect weapons, explosives, and the passengers who would try to smuggle them aboard was, and still is, essential to aviation security. The techniques used to detect explosives in airports today are X-ray machines and magnetometers. X rays are used to screen cargo and luggage for bomb shapes. The magnetometer, a sort of door frame through which a passenger steps, detects metal carried on a person.

Due mostly to the effectiveness of these methods, airplane hijackings decreased in the 1980s. In place of guns and easy-to-detect explosives, however, terrorists began making bombs with plastic explosives. Semtex, the explosive used in the Pan Am 103 bombing, is an especially powerful plastic explosive. Semtex has the consistency of dough: It can be molded to fit into radios or cassette players, or folded into thin, paper-like sheets and slipped into luggage. It is extremely difficult to detect with X rays because it does not look like a bomb. It cannot be detected by magnetometer either, because Semtex and other plastic explosives have no metal content.

Terrorists have access to Semtex in large quantities. Vaclav Havel, president of Czechoslovakia, where the explosive is made, said recently that under the previous regime his country exported a thousand tons of Semtex to Libya. Only a small amount of Semtex is needed to destroy a jumbo jet, and Havel estimated that the world terrorist community had enough of the explosive to make bombs for the next 150 years.

Traditional methods of detection are no longer able to ensure the safety of those who fly, and new technologies are urgently needed. Devices designed to detect plastic explosives are already being tested at some airports, and scientists continue to work on researching and developing other methods.

X-ray machines are used to scan luggage at Kennedy Airport, New York. These machines were introduced in the 1960s and 1970s to combat terrorism.

Semtex explosives are carefully hidden within these calculators.

Semtex, a powerful, hard-to-detect plastic explosive, the bomb had moved through airport security in a suitcase.

More Bomb Attempts

There were more terrorist attempts in 1986. On April 17, terrorists tried and failed to put a bomb on board an Israeli El-Al jet in London. On June 26, a suitcase carrying a bomb caused minor damage when it exploded early at a terminal in Madrid.

The international airline industry felt the effects of increased terrorism. People feared flying, and the airlines saw business slip. One airline, Pan Am, wanted to convince people that its airline was safe. It hired a consulting firm, KPI, which assigned analyst Isaac Yeffet the task of reviewing Pan Am's security system.

Yeffet knew about terrorists and airplanes. A former security chief for Israeli airline El-Al, he had developed a comprehensive security system in response to frequent terrorist attacks on El-Al flights. After reviewing Pan Am's security operations, Yeffet presented his findings in a confidential report that went straight to the point. "Pan Am is highly vulnerable to most forms of terrorist attack," he wrote. Yeffet criticized Pan Am for relying too heavily on X-ray machines, which cannot detect every kind of explosive. He recommended hand searches which would be more thorough. Further, Yeffet reported, Pan Am was ineffective at identifying suspicious passengers

and questioning them. Finally, the airline failed to regularly test its own procedures.

Yeffet had singled out the Frankfurt Main Airport, where Flight 103 originated before continuing onto the Heathrow, writing that "a bomb would have a good chance of getting through security" there. If Pan Am wanted to avoid a major disaster, he warned, it would have to restructure its whole security system. Yeffet made a frightening conclusion: "Pan Am is almost totally vulnerable to a midair explosion through explosive charges concealed in the cargo."

Pan Am Fails Security Tests

Despite Yeffet's warnings, Pan Am believed it could fix the problem without making substantial changes or purchasing expensive new equip-

Isaac Yeffet was hired by Pan Am to review its security procedures. Even though Yeffet had recommended drastic changes in security, Pan Am took little action.

Security dogs at San Francisco National Airport attempt to sniff out explosives. Similar dogs were used by Pan Am to create an atmosphere of safety at JFK Airport. Unfortunately, the dogs were only well-behaved German shepherds.

ment. In 1986, the airline started its own security system, Alert Management Systems, Inc. It devoted approximately $18 million a year to the new project, raising the money in part by charging passengers an extra five dollars on transatlantic-flight tickets. But even with more funds, Alert did little to improve security, according to critics. They contended that the airline cared more about creating the appearance of safety than about making changes to ensure passenger safety. To announce its new safety program at New York's JFK Airport, Alert paraded dogs in front of the check-in counter. What viewers thought were trained bomb-sniffing dogs were really only well-behaved German shepherds leased from a local kennel.

The dogs were not alone in lack-ing specialized training. Alert's chief of security at Frankfurt Main was twenty-nine-year-old Ulrich Weber, who had a criminal record in the United States for writing bad checks. He also had a habit of hiring unqualified workers. He hired Sabine Fuchs, who, as a screener, had the important task of discovering whether any passengers fit the profile of a terrorist. Her job involved questioning people to find out if they might be carrying guns or bombs onto the plane. She had no training or experience in the field, however; her last job had been as a hairdresser. Another employee, Simone Keller, also had no experience in the job she had been assigned; four days after being hired she was promoted to supervisor. Why? "Mr. Weber told me I had wonderful blue eyes," she said.

Then in fall 1988, two years after Alert started operation, the FAA (Federal Aviation Administration) conducted a routine check and found flaws in Pan Am's security at the Frankfurt Airport. Alert had failed to track suspicious passengers. It had also failed to track interline baggage—the bags transferred from one airplane to another—to make sure it was X-rayed. Under such lax security conditions, it was possible for a bag with a bomb in it to be slipped, undetected, among other bags. In November the Alert program at Heathrow Airport tested its own system by planting a weapon in a piece of luggage; it cleared security without a problem.

Alert's first president, Fred Ford, knew the program's flaws from the start. According to Ford, Alert's hiring practices were part of the trouble. "I felt that any system that [had] . . . a group of employees that took their job[s] no more seriously than flipping hamburgers at McDonald's was not a very good system," he said. Ford felt so strongly that, in July 1988, he wrote a confidential memo to his supervisors at Pan Am. In it, he complained that Alert had failed to live up to its advertised promises and that security remained inadequate. Not long after, Ford was dismissed from his job.

Image Seemed More Important

As the terrorist threat continued to grow, Pan Am still seemed more concerned about its image than about improving security. Alert's

vice president for operations, Wilfred Wood, noted, "Security wasn't of prime importance to Pan Am; on-time performance was of prime importance to Pan Am." On-time performance is rated by how many flights depart on schedule. When an airline increases security measures by questioning suspicious passengers or searching through luggage, departure times can be delayed.

Pan Am officials were understandably worried about losing business to delays. But in order to please customers, they underestimated the danger posed by terrorism. An internal memo written by a Pan Am official in October 1988—a time when tension over terrorism was at a peak—announced that "for financial reasons, the security staff has to

Fred Ford was Alert's first president. When Ford wrote a confidential memo criticizing Alert's procedures, he was dismissed from his job.

19

Ahmed Jibril (left), leader of the Popular Front for the Liberation of Palestine, a Middle Eastern terrorist group. Jibril's group had been caught with bomb-making equipment similar to that used in the Lockerbie bomb.

be kept to a minimum."

As Pan Am struggled to balance security needs with customers' needs, terrorist groups were becoming a presence in Europe. Terrorists found it easier to stage attacks in Europe than in the Middle East. In autumn 1988, West German secret police, the BKA, were watching the movements of a group called the PFLP-GC (Popular Front for the Liberation of Palestine—General Command) as they established an operations base in West Germany.

The PFLP-GC has been active in the Middle East for many years. The group's leader, Ahmed Jibril, is a Palestinian. Jibril and other Palestinians are in conflict with Israelis because both claim the same area in the Middle East as their homeland. Jibril and his organization are extremists who believe they must completely destroy the state of Israel to reclaim Palestine as their homeland. They commit acts of violence against Israel and its supporters, including the United States. At a 1986 press conference in Libya, Jibril made an ominous pronouncement: "There will be no safety for any traveler on an Israeli or U.S. airliner."

The BKA knew that the PFLP-GC had rented apartments in West Germany and that group members came and went from the rooms at all hours. For several weeks the BKA had been closely observing them. Israeli intelligence had warned the BKA that Jibril's followers or another extremist group might attempt to bomb an American airliner departing from the Frankfurt airport. The Israelis believed that the terrorists might strike late in 1988.

The BKA tapped the telephones of PFLP-GC members and followed them as they shopped for electronic devices. They overheard a call from a man they knew to be a bomb maker in which he said he had "made some changes in the medicine" and that it was "better and stronger than before." After weeks of watching, the BKA decided to attempt to arrest PFLP-GC members and confiscate the bombs. On October 26, in a sweep of apartments and businesses across Germany, they arrested sixteen men.

A State-of-the-Art Bomb

BKA agents could not believe what they found. One of the apartments they searched stored enough weapons to arm a small army. A bazooka, a grenade launcher, thirty hand grenades, six rifles, ample ammunition, and explosives such as Semtex, TNT, and dynamite were all confiscated by the BKA. The BKA also succeeded in arresting Jibril's assistant and a bomb maker in the terrorists' car. In the back seat, beneath a blanket, agents found a Toshiba cassette player. On closer inspection, they discovered a state-of-the-art bomb hidden inside the tape player. The bomb was made for one purpose only: to blow up a plane in midair.

Unfortunately, the very next day, the BKA released all but three of the men, strangely enough, for lack of evidence. The police could not link the men to a specific crime, though they knew for certain some of the men were dangerous terrorists. Police were able, however, to keep the seized weapons, which included the makings of deadly terrorist bombs. They displayed them at a press conference, where they announced they had prevented a major terrorist attack. What they did not know was that they had failed to confiscate all the bombs.

Three weeks after the incident, the Federal Aviation Administration released a security alert informing all airlines of the tape-player bomb. The bulletin described the Toshiba cassette bomb in detail, warning that it was "nearly impossible to detect through normal inspection procedures." But a Pan Am worker at Frankfurt Main Airport whose job it was to post security bulletins never received the warning. This meant that baggage-inspection employees never heard they were supposed to be on the lookout for a cassette-player bomb.

A Serious Message

Then, late in the morning of December 5, the American embassy in Helsinki, Finland, received a phone call from a man with a thick Arab accent and a serious message. Sometime in the next few weeks, he said, a terrorist organization would try to smuggle a bomb onto a Pan Am flight from Frankfurt to the United States. The caller would not give his name or say where he got his information. When the embassy employee taking the call pressed him for details, the caller hung up.

The embassy informed Pan Am of the call, and the airline immediately sent Alan Berwick, a senior security official, to Helsinki to investigate. There, Finnish intelligence officials told Berwick the call had been a hoax. They knew of the caller, they said, and had been watching him for weeks. He had called in bomb threats to the Israeli embassy, as well. Finnish officials investigated the man and found he had no connection to terrorist groups. Al-

though his antics were strange, his bomb threats were empty.

Just to be safe, Berwick wrote a confidential memo to Alert personnel to place "special emphasis on the handling of interline baggage at Frankfurt." But Alert chief of security Ulrich Weber failed to distribute the memo to his staff.

When they boarded Flight 103 on the evening of December 21, passengers had no inkling of the threats to their safety. Just two months before, PFLP-GC terrorists had been arrested in Frankfurt with a bomb made for blowing up airplanes; most of them had been released. Although BKA officials confiscated a bomb, they did not know others had been made. They did know that the bomb the terrorists designed, with

Semtex explosive, which was used in the Lockerbie bomb, is easily hidden and difficult to detect. Here, the explosive has been placed in a book.

its barometric fuse and Toshiba tape-player exterior, would be "nearly impossible to detect" through normal inspection means.

Passengers were also unaware that just a week before a man had called in a bomb threat for a Pan Am flight to America sometime in December. Though the call was dismissed as a hoax, the threat was taken seriously enough to prompt officials at the American Embassy in Moscow to post the threat publicly so employees could change their flight plans if they wished.

Finally, passengers remained unaware that throughout November and December, the FAA had sent a number of security bulletins warning air carriers and airports to step up security measures because of increasing terrorist threats. Some of these warnings had not made it to Alert security staff in Frankfurt.

The passengers on Flight 103 remained blissfully unaware of any of the events that would soon conspire to change their destinies. They were simply eager to get home. They had no idea they would never get there.

Three

Disaster Strikes

It had been a busy day for the controllers at the Scottish Air Traffic Control Centre in Prestwick on the southwest coast of Scotland. Driving winds had made it necessary to re-route the flight paths of large planes flying overseas, and that meant more air traffic than usual. Close to 7:00 P.M., Alan Topp, an air-traffic controller for eighteen years, took an incoming message from Captain MacQuarrie on board Flight 103.

"Clipper one-zero-three," Mac-Quarrie radioed. "We are level at three-one-zero."

The pilot was identifying Pan Am Flight 103 and telling flight control that he had reached his cruising altitude of thirty-one thousand feet. Topp checked 103's identification code, confirmed the plane's position and altitude, and instructed MacQuarrie to take the 747 over

Lockerbie.

Then Topp studied his radar screen, where he could see Flight 103 inch forward, a bright green cross inside a tiny box. He turned away from the screen for a moment to talk to a London shuttle pilot who was requesting permission to descend. When he looked back, the tiny green box still moved across his screen. And then, suddenly, it was gone.

The green box simply vanished, and where it had been were four or five little blinking boxes. "It struck me immediately," Topp said later, "that they looked like Christmas tree lights because they were winking. In a sense, they were twinkling." Shortly after, the boxes disappeared altogether, leaving only a blank screen.

Immediately Topp tried to contact the plane. "Clipper one-zero-three." No answer. He tried again, but heard only silence. Something was not right. Topp called across the room to his shift manager, but the manager was listening intently to his headphones: The pilot of the London shuttle was reporting that he had witnessed a fiery explosion on the ground. Topp felt ill as he guessed the awful truth.

Blown to Bits

Pan Am Flight 103 had just been blown to bits. Bodies, great hunks of blazing metal, and other debris began to shower down on Lockerbie.

It was 7:03 P.M. At that moment, the seismographs at the Earthquake Monitoring Center in Dumfries-shire, some fourteen miles from

The cockpit of the ill-fated *Maid of the Seas.* An air traffic controller at the busy Scottish Air Traffic Control Centre in Scotland witnessed the crash on his radar screen.

HOW DOES RADAR WORK?

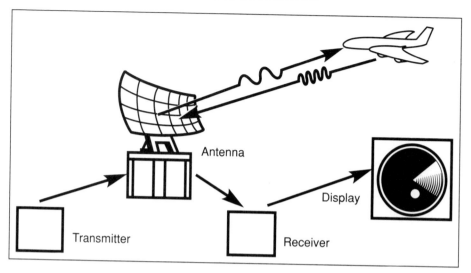

Antenna

Display

Transmitter

Receiver

Radar is an electronic instrument that detects and locates moving or fixed objects. Ships and aircraft rely heavily on radar because it allows them to "see" through heavy fog, rain, or snow and to operate at night. Radar can also determine the direction, distance, height, and speed of objects as far as planets and their moons.

A radar set works by sending out radio waves toward an object and receiving the waves that bounce back. The object's range—its distance from the radar set—is determined by how long it takes for the reflected waves to return. The object's location is determined by the direction from which the waves return.

What a radar operator actually sees is a dark screen with illuminated dots, or blips, representing objects. Those blips are the result of a sequence that begins with a transmitter, which produces radar waves, and an antenna, which sends them out. The same antenna usually collects the waves bounced back from an object. The returning waves, or echoes, are then strengthened by a receiver so they can be seen on a display screen. The echoes appear as blips of light on the screen. The radio waves themselves are actually electromagnetic waves trav-

eling at the speed of light—186,282 miles per second.

Modern aircraft use various types of radar to aid pilots. Radar altimeter, for example, shows a pilot how high the plane is flying. Weather radar detects nearby storms, alerting pilots to rough conditions so that they can change course if possible. Radar also allows planes to avoid collisions: Air-traffic controllers can direct an airport's constant flow of incoming and outgoing planes so that each flies a separate path. Using radar, controllers can see the position of every plane in the sky within at least fifty miles of the airport.

Air-traffic controller Alan Topp knew something unusual had happened to Pan Am Flight 103 when it disappeared from his radar screen. He had been following its movements when the tiny green blip representing the plane suddenly broke into four or five blinking lights. The next moment all the blips vanished. Radar had actually detected the plane's explosion. What was once one object had become several to the radar. The falling fragments of the aircraft quickly disintegrated into pieces too small and too low for the controller's radar to detect, and the display lost the flight altogether.

Lockerbie, measured 1.9 on the Richter scale. The tremor had been caused by Flight 103's crash to earth.

Fire Raining from the Sky

Lockerbie resident Ian Good was in his kitchen making dinner when he heard strange sounds. "I shut the kitchen door, thinking it would be thunder and lightning, then I realized it was too cold and windy for that. Then the noise seemed to get louder and louder. The cat flap in the door started to flap and the walls vibrated and the crockery on the draining board shook. I thought it was an earthquake. I went to the door to look and at that moment the noise stopped." He could see flames in the sky about half a mile away.

To Ella Ramsden, sitting before her fireplace in the living room, the noise was terrible. "It got louder and louder and the whole house started to shake," she remembered. She looked out her window and saw that the sky was bright orange. She thought she should get out of the house, so she scooped up Cara, her dog, and hurried toward her kitchen door. As she struggled to open it, the lights went out and the shaking resumed, this time more violently. The walls of her house were collapsing.

"There was this terrible swell of wind, which brought up the dust, whooshing, whooshing. I was being sucked back into the house. My legs were hurting as dust and dirt were sucked in past me. Then there was a

Flight 103's crash was so large, it was recorded by seismographs fourteen miles away.

terrible quietness which I will never forget. I looked up, and from where I was standing, I could see the sky and the stars."

The neighbors came running to the front of Ramsden's house, and when they saw the destruction, they were sure she could not have survived. Rubble and airplane wreckage were strewn everywhere; what looked like a section of fuselage lay in the garden. But they heard her cries for help. They ran to the back, where part of the house still stood, and helped Ramsden through the debris, amazed to find her unhurt.

Ramsden and her neighbors looked around them in disbelief. What moments before had been a peaceful backyard garden where

here and there a plant still struggled, was now a scene of death. On Ramsden's roof lay the body of a young woman, still strapped into her airplane seat. Over the next few days, seventy more bodies would be recovered from the devastated remains of her home and garden.

In the garage of David Edward's home in Sherwood Crescent, in the southwest end of town, David and Stephen Flannigan were just putting the tire back on Joanne Flannigan's bike when they heard rumbling. "It's thunder," Stephen told David. They were not so sure, though, when they saw the overhead strip light start to fall from the ceiling. Through the garage doors, they saw pieces of wreckage fall out of the sky and knew it was a plane. When the whole garage started to shake, the boys darted into the street. They saw people fleeing burning homes. Stephen wondered what was happening at his own house, half a block away.

As it happened, Sherwood Crescent was the part of town most devastated by the plane crash. There, the jumbo jet's huge engines and the wings containing the fuel tanks crashed to earth, landing on homes that lined the street. The impact gouged a deep crater in the earth and sent an exploding fireball three

A great gouge of earth and wrecked houses in Lockerbie shows the path taken by the crashing Pan Am Flight 103.

Police try to identify victims of Flight 103. The search for evidence extended over hundreds of miles.

hundred feet into the air. A gas main ruptured, adding fuel to already roaring fires. The raging flames engulfed anything that could burn—trees and bushes, cars, and buildings.

The Reverend Alan Neil was visiting friends in Sherwood Crescent when the wings of the airplane swept overhead. As they hit the ground, the house trembled. "I went outside," he said, "and saw that my car was on fire. There was black smoke coming from houses. They were burning like an inferno within two minutes. There was nothing we could do."

At the center of the explosion, where the heat was most intense, homes and the people in them had vaporized, disappearing without a trace. Several unsuspecting residents of Lockerbie died in their own homes. In the first hours after the crash, the extent of the destruction made it impossible to tell how many townspeople had lost their lives, but estimates put the number at twenty-two.

Police attempted to account for those who lived in the most badly damaged areas of town. They went door to door, registering the names of residents. At 10:00 P.M. they posted lists of the known survivors on the doors of the town hall, adding to the lists during the night. Anxious friends and relatives of the missing gathered outside the hall, scanning the lists for the names of

29

The body of a passenger, still strapped to an airline seat, is lowered by a rescue worker.

their loved ones.

The whereabouts of many of those missing were determined over the next few days. Some had been away on vacation or visiting friends in town. Some had fled their homes in panic. But others had not been so lucky. Stephen Flannigan would learn that his family—his mother, father, and sister—had perished while he had stepped out to repair a bicycle tire. Their neighbors, the Somerville family were gone, too—John and Rosaleen and their two children, Paul, 13, and Lyndsey, 10. None of their bodies could be found.

"A Terrible Explosion"

The powerful stench of aviation fuel hung in the air in Sherwood Crescent. A local man who had been driving past the neighborhood gas station when the plane crashed described the horrific scene: "There was a terrible explosion and the whole sky lit up and the sky was actually raining fire. It was just like liquid." Another eyewitness said it was like "hell on earth," with homes on fire and people screaming and running through the streets.

The plane had landed within yards of the A74, the main road that runs through Lockerbie and connects Scotland to England. The fiery crash stopped traffic and ignited cars. One truck driver stomped on his brakes as the fireball exploded twenty-five yards from him and red-hot wreckage pelted his truck. "I saw one of the drivers leap from his car as it was shredded by debris," he said. "He got clear and then it burst into flames." Another man driving on the A74 said, "It was like a bomb going up." He saw people stagger from the burning houses nearby, and he helped them to safety.

Wreckage from the plane reached to the outskirts of Lockerbie, too. Jimmie and June Wilson were drinking coffee at their farmhouse three miles from town when their lights went out. Outside they noticed a hulking shape at the far end of the fields; it was the *Maid of the Seas'* cockpit. Its lights still glowed, and the Wilsons approached it hopefully. But they found no survivors. MacQuarrie's body had been ejected and lay outside the cockpit. Three more crew members' bodies remained inside. Despite all the damage, the cockpit lights glowed on, powered by an emergency generator.

Thousands of pieces of debris lay strewn across the fields: luggage, sections of aircraft, battered Christmas presents. And bodies were everywhere. Some were badly mangled. Others looked as if they were simply asleep. Many were half-dressed, the clothing having been torn from their bodies in the five-mile drop from the sky. Their bodies sank into the soggy Scottish earth where they landed.

Shortly after the jet crashed, Chief Constable John Boyd, the head of Lockerbie's tiny twenty-two member police force, realized he had a major disaster on his hands. He immediately set the town of Lockerbie into action. Every available fire truck, ambulance, and police car sped to the disaster site. Boyd knew that, although police forces from neighboring towns could help, they would not be enough. He invoked his special authority to call on the military for assistance.

Soldiers Leave for Lockerbie

At army bases across Scotland and England, hundreds of soldiers prepared to leave for Lockerbie. Helicopters flew out from surrounding air force bases. Through the night, some five hundred soldiers and police officers made the trip to Lockerbie to aid the rescue effort. Boyd spread out a map of Lockerbie, marked off six search areas, and sent workers to each.

Helicopters crisscrossed the skies

Children in Lockerbie survey the wreckage of the Pan Am crash.

above the search grids, tracing with bright searchlights the path of devastation left by the fallen jet. Any survivors would have to be found quickly or they would die of exposure in the cold weather. The Lockerbie town hall was set up as a temporary medical clinic. Hospitals across western Scotland went on emergency standby, preparing to treat hundreds of casualties.

Volunteers, too, appeared from all over the country to help. A mountain rescue team arrived with specially trained dogs to locate survivors of airplane crashes in rugged mountain areas. Town residents streamed from their homes to help however they could. Several gathered at the community center, where they brought hot coffee and food for weary rescue workers. Others ventured out into the cold night with the other searchers, hoping to find the injured as quickly as possible.

From Medical Clinic to Morgue

But these efforts would prove to be in vain. There was no one to rescue. Among all the horrible wreckage, workers found only lifeless bodies. Within hours, the town hall was converted from a medical clinic to a

A member of the mountain rescue team helps search out crash victims in Lockerbie. The remains of the cockpit lie in the background.

32

morgue. By 2:20 A.M. the rescue co-ordination center at Edinburgh reported, "A rescue situation does not exist anymore—we are just recovering bodies."

As it turned out, only twelve people, all of them from Sherwood Crescent, needed medical care. All 259 people on board Pan Am Flight 103 died. Eleven more died on the ground at Lockerbie, bringing the number of dead to 270. By any measure, it was a terrible tragedy.

Word Reaches the Relatives

About an hour after the crash, relatives who had begun arriving at JFK Airport in New York intending to pick up family members heard, instead, the terrible news of the fatal crash. "We don't have a daughter anymore," sobbed Susan Cohen, as she and her husband, Daniel, learned that the plane carrying Theodora Cohen, the drama student returning from London, had exploded. Dodging television cameras ready to record their grief, family members made their way to a lounge Pan Am had reserved for them. Emergency-service chaplain Frank Rafter was there, trying to soothe relatives who arrived not knowing the news. A woman whose son had been on board the ill-fated flight threw herself into the chaplain's arms, crying "He was just twenty-one on Monday."

Word of the disaster spread quickly. Some rushed to the airport after seeing news of it on television. Relatives began arriving at Heathrow Airport in London, too. Social workers and chaplains offered comfort to the anguished families of the victims.

Pan Am knew there had been no survivors from the plane, but before they could contact relatives, they

---

COULD ANYONE HAVE SURVIVED FLIGHT 103?

Two passengers aboard Flight 103 may have survived the fall from thirty-one thousand feet, according to a pathologist who testified before a fatal accident inquiry in Dumfries, Scotland.

"The chances are that, even if they had survived, they would have been deeply unconscious after sustaining their injuries," said Dr. Anthony Bussuttil. Bussuttil is a professor of forensic medicine at Edinburgh University who testified before the inquiry on October 17, 1990.

Bussuttil told investigators that eight pathologists grouped the victims into three categories: the majority of passengers who most likely died immediately from injuries; a smaller number with less-severe injuries but whose vital organs were extensively damaged, causing immediate death or unconsciousness; and two passengers with less-severe injuries.

"It is possible that this third group may have survived for a short time," Bussuttil said. When asked if one or both might have survived given the "best qualified medical team possible," Bussuttil replied: "There is a possibility that, if resuscitation was available immediately with access to hospital facilities, there could have been survival."

Bussuttil pointed out that, given the plane's altitude when it exploded, the victims' 2-1/2-minute free fall would have reached speeds of about 120 miles per hour. "Some victims may have fallen faster because they were attached to heavy parts of the aircraft," he explained. "Some may have fallen more slowly because they were with parts of the aircraft which fluttered down."

British prime minister Margaret Thatcher (right) walks away from the wreckage of the crumpled cockpit of Pan Am Flight 103.

needed to verify the names of Flight 103's passengers. Communication between Lockerbie and the airports made this difficult. It was 10:30 P.M. (EST) before Pan Am officials could confirm the fate of loved ones for anxious relatives.

World leaders sent their condolences to Lockerbie. President Ronald Reagan wrote to city officials, "Our hearts go out to you on this tragic occasion, which marred what should have been a season of joy." Soviet president Mikhail Gorbachev relayed his sympathy to British prime minister Margaret Thatcher. Thatcher paid a visit to the town herself the morning following the crash and was given a helicopter tour of the wreckage sites.

Clearly moved by the destruction and great number of bodies being carried from the fields, she addressed the townspeople and spoke about her own feelings of shock and grief. She had already sent a message of sympathy to President Reagan. "It is not only terrible for the people of this town and for Scotland," she explained, "but for United States citizens, as most of the people on board are their people."

What had been planned as a massive rescue effort soon became a massive search effort, as workers tagged bodies and combed through debris for any clues that might help to explain the crash. Their task was enormous. Because the airplane had been traveling at 550 miles per hour when it broke apart, the wreckage spread far and wide. In a village five miles from Lockerbie, a man stepped outside to investigate a crash he had heard and found a ten-foot-high piece of fuselage sticking up in his field. Another man reported a body strapped to a plane seat in his yard, ten miles from Lockerbie.

Strong winds carried lighter items from inside the plane even farther. Mailbags from the flight were found thirty miles away in the town of Northumberland. Debris scattered in a wide arc across the border area between England and Scotland and as far as the North Sea, seventy miles away. A watch torn from a body that fell in a Lockerbie field was discovered in a village eighty miles away. In the early hours the search expanded to include locations over one hundred miles away. Later, it would have to extend much farther.

The Awful Truth

One more point seemed clear from the onset: Constable Boyd and other investigators immediately suspected that the crash of Flight 103 had not been an accident. Huge 747s did not just fall from the sky. The nature of the damage suggested that a bomb brought the plane down, but investigators would have to find solid evidence that could be tested at a crime lab to be absolutely

Aircraft seats from the downed 747.

sure. If it turned out the disaster had been the calculated work of a terrorist organization, the authorities would have a criminal investigation on their hands.

For that reason, the search had to be absolutely thorough. Boyd ordered that every body be treated as a potential murder victim. Every piece of debris was a vital clue to be documented, every body was invaluable evidence for a possible future trial. All those involved with the investigation felt the same way: If this was murder, it was murder on a massive scale. Those responsible must be brought to justice.

Four

The Investigation Begins

As the long terrible night turned into day, the chaos and confusion of the early hours following the crash slowly gave way. Firefighters managed to control the raging fires in Sherwood Crescent. Police and search workers continued to recover bodies from the hillsides around Lockerbie. By noon they had retrieved nearly 150 of them. In the grim light of the morning after, the damage looked awful. Wreckage was visible everywhere.

A brief helicopter tour told Constable Boyd that he would have to extend the search areas yet again. Meanwhile, search workers continued to pour into town. By the day after the crash, December 22, more than a thousand police officers and six hundred military personnel had arrived in Lockerbie. The first stage of what would be a far-reaching investigation had begun to take hold.

That morning, the question on every mind was the same: What had caused Flight 103 to fall out of the sky? The plane disappeared from radar at thirty-one thousand feet without so much as an emergency call. Whatever went wrong had happened instantly. Captain MacQuarrie had never even had time to respond.

According to investigators from the U.S. National Transportation Safety Board, all three communications radios and the plane's two transponders went dead at exactly the same second. That meant there had been an instantaneous and total loss of power to the cockpit, the aviation experts described it as an "explosive decompression." Experts agreed there were only three events that could cause such a complete power loss: a midair collision, a massive structural failure, or a bomb.

The Third Possibility

The first option could be ruled out immediately. There had been no midair collision. Most of the investigators suspected the third possibility, that a bomb had brought the plane down. Nevertheless, they could not dismiss the possibility of massive structural failure. After all, the *Maid of the Seas* was one of the oldest jumbo jets still flying. Built in 1970, only the fifteenth 747 made by Boeing, the airplane had logged a lot of hours since then.

FAA records revealed the plane had a history of difficulties. Since

The reconstructed forward cargo hold of Flight 103 shows the effects of the blast that caused the crash.

1980 it had experienced twenty-one mechanical problems. Corrosion had caused cracks in the fuselage. A wing flap had once fallen from the plane during takeoff from Karachi, Pakistan. But in 1987, the plane had spent six months being overhauled in a Kansas repair facility. The plane's structure, the engines, and the landing gear had all been checked. According to a Boeing spokesperson, all the problems listed in the FAA report would have been corrected during those months of repair.

Even if structural failure seemed the less likely possibility, no one could state with certainty that a bomb had caused the crash without evidence to prove it beyond a doubt. In the beginning, no one knew for sure what had happened. But investigators were not wasting any time in trying to find out.

Meanwhile, those whose lives were personally affected by the crash were coping as best they could. Syracuse University canceled final exams to hold a memorial service for the thirty-five students who had lost their lives. Families of American crash victims began traveling to Lockerbie. Pan Am offered to fly family members of the 192 Americans aboard Flight 103 to Lockerbie to begin the process of identifying loved ones and bringing them home. The first group of relatives left the United States on the evening of December 22, and over the next few days, several more followed.

These families were welcome to Lockerbie by residents who were themselves struggling with the aftermath of the tragedy. Many had been left homeless and were lodged temporarily with relatives or in local hotels already burdened by the crowds of reporters who had descended on Lockerbie.

Coping with the Grief

Within days, teams of social workers had been assigned to a long-term counseling project to help those affected cope with their grief. According to a social-services director, serious problems would continue to arise as Lockerbie came to terms with the full impact of the disaster. Counselors were preparing for months or even years of treatment for victims' relatives and friends.

A Syracuse University student clutches a hymnbook as she sits with other students during a memorial service for the university students killed on Flight 103.

In spite of their own troubles Lockerbie residents showed great warmth and compassion to the Americans who had come to be where their loved ones had died. A strong sense of community filled the town as survivors shared their stories and their grief over coffee at the civic center. On Christmas Day, people of all denominations gathered together in the town's churches before returning to the depressing business of identifying their loved ones' bodies and belongings.

Thousands of Details

The rapidly growing investigation team needed a central post from which to operate, so the town's school, Lockerbie Academy, became a headquarters. Officials from several British and American agencies, including the FBI, the CIA, the FAA, and the British Air Accident Investigation Branch, set up offices there and a newly installed computer system tracked the thousands of details concerning the case. Large-scale maps of the search areas hung on the walls.

Finding evidence of a bomb explosion among the wreckage would not be easy, but Constable Boyd had plenty of assistance. He and chief investigator John Orr worked closely with a team of explosives experts and forensic specialists. Their first step was to advise search workers to collect every bit of aircraft and luggage debris they could find. Any piece of wreckage—no matter how small or insignificant look-

Lockerbie Academy became the investigation headquarters after the crash.

ing—might bear traces of explosive matter, and Boyd stressed the importance of thoroughness in the search. He told workers, "If it's not a rock and it's not growing, pick it up and put it in a bag."

Ultimately, the search extended to eleven sections covering 845 square miles. Search workers combed through bogs, fields, and forests, collecting evidence of the crash in large plastic bags. Their task seemed overwhelming. Plane debris was strewn through the largest forest in Great Britain, Kiedler Forest, where the trees were so thick, wreckage that helicopter pilots spotted in treetops could not be seen from the ground. But the searchers worked diligently, to the point even of crawling on their hands and knees at times. They seemed to miss nothing. When an FAA official who was inspecting a search area lost his hearing aid in the tall wet grass of a Scottish bog, he did not expect to see it again. Just four days later it showed up, in a bag of debris collected by the searchers.

Looking for Tiny Dents

In the field outside Lockerbie where the cockpit had fallen to earth, investigators spent hours scrutinizing every piece of electrical wire, every scrap of twisted metal. They were looking in particular for pieces of metal or luggage with tiny dents in them. When a bomb ex-

A police officer examines a recovered passenger seat for clues to the cause of the Lockerbie crash.

plodes in the pressurized cabin of an airplane, it sends fragments of itself and anything surrounding it hurtling outward at a speed of twenty-four thousand feet per second. These fragments become embedded in nearby surfaces, leaving tiny dents of a certain depth. By measuring the dents, scientists can determine with certainty if they were made by an exploding bomb.

Investigators also looked for the tiny burn marks a bomb will leave on surrounding objects, as well as for traces of Semtex or some other explosive. Because these traces might be found on the skin of crash victims, or victims' injuries might suggest the presence of explosives, the bodies had to be treated as evidence, too. They were examined where they lay, and some were subjected to tests. As a result, recovery of bodies from the fields was often slow, adding to the pain and anger relatives felt. Although police sympathized with the families, they had received strict orders to treat every victim as potentially crucial evidence.

A Laborious Process

Search workers brought clothing and luggage debris to a chemical warehouse temporarily used to store crash evidence. After undergoing X-ray examinations, the materials were given to explosives experts who decided what to send to the crime lab for further testing. Materials not sent on were handed to other officers, who tagged each item and entered it on the com-

Searchers painstakingly went over every inch of ground in Lockerbie. Here, members of the Royal Air Force examine the tail section from the plane.

puter system. Finally, after every item had been photographed, it was sorted into piles from which relatives could claim belongings. The process was laborious, but every article from the plane had to be accounted for.

On Christmas Day the investigation's painstaking attention paid off. A searcher crossing a field picked up a metal fragment with telltale marks in it. Someone else found a piece of luggage with rips and tears that could have been made by flying metal. These pieces were taken to the Royal Armaments Research and Development Establishment, a British military crime lab that is one of the best in the world. Specialists ran tests on the materials, and on December 26 they were able to confirm what so many already privately believed: A bomb had indeed blown up Flight 103.

Which Terrorist?

Once they knew that, investigators turned to the next important question. Who had placed the bomb on board, and why? Every possible suspect would have to be taken into account. In this case, that made for an unusually high number. All 259 people on Flight 103 had to be considered potential suspects. A baggage handler or a maintenance worker could have slipped the bomb on board, so any airport

CLUES IN THE WRECKAGE

If a bomb did destroy Flight 103, investigators knew there would be evidence. It was simply a matter of being able to find it among all the wreckage and debris. Years of research have shown that if a bomb explodes in an aircraft, fragments of it are hurled into surrounding objects at twenty-four thousand feet per second, ten times faster than if the jet broke apart due to a collision, for example. These fragments "stick to their depth" in whatever objects they strike—scientists call this "high-speed particle penetration"—leaving tiny dents that can be measured in a laboratory. If investigators found pieces of metal or luggage with dents of a certain depth, they would have proof that a bomb caused the explosion.

Scientists might also find traces of burns or soot from explosives on items from the plane or even on victims' bodies. The traces could possibly tell what kind of explosive was used.

Investigators were also looking for what is referred to as the black box, which is actually painted bright orange so it can be easily spotted among wreckage. The black box consists of a flight-data recorder, which monitors every movement of the plane, and a cockpit voice recorder, which captures all conversation between the pilot and air-traffic control. When the tapes are played back, a computer can make a "fingerprint" of the noise in the cabin, that allows its sound patterns to be compared to recordings of known explosions.

A policeman guards the hangar where workers sift through the wreckage of Flight 103.

personnel who had access to the plane would have to be interviewed. That included workers in Los Angeles and San Francisco, where Flight 103 had stopped before arriving in London. Airport personnel at Heathrow and Frankfurt would also need to be questioned. The number of potential suspects came to over a thousand people, according to Bob Ricks, an FBI official involved with the Lockerbie investigation.

The FBI began dispatching agents around the United States and abroad to handle the considerable task of interviewing airport workers and the family and friends of victims. Every suspect's name had to be cleared to ensure a thorough investigation.

Terrorists Suspected

Despite these procedures, some investigators suspected immediately that terrorists were behind the bombing. Just fifteen hours after the crash, a telephone call seemed to support that suspicion. A man called the London offices of two news agencies, Associated Press and United Press International, claiming to speak for a group called Guardians of the Islamic Revolution. The group had blown up Pan Am 103, he claimed, to avenge the shooting down of an Iran Air plane some months earlier.

Terrorism and intelligence experts in Washington, D.C., had never heard of an organization called the Guardians of the Islamic Revolution. They were quite sure, in fact, that it did not exist. They knew that terrorists often use code names as a way to spread confusion about their activities, and they suspected the call was meant to do that. Still, it might be worth something as a clue. Although the call did not point to the perpetrator, it did suggest a likely motive: revenge against the United States for a tragic accident.

The accident occurred six months before, on July 3, 1988. At the time, Iran and Iraq were at war. U.S. battleships patrolled the Persian Gulf, protecting oil tankers passing through the straits from Iranian attack. A crew member on the warship U.S.S. *Vincennes* spotted what he thought was an Iranian F-14 fighter plane on the ship's radar, and informed Capt. Will Rogers III. Believing the *Vincennes* to be in danger, Rogers gave orders to shoot the plane down. It turned out that the aircraft was not a fighter plane at all, however, but an Iranian commercial airliner carrying shoppers to the city of Dubai. On board were 277 adults and 63 children. All of them died.

Israelis Sound Warning

Some Iranians believed the United States had known the plane was a commercial airliner, but had it shot down anyway. Various intelligence officials feared terrorists might retaliate on behalf of Iran. Israelis warned West Germany that terrorists might try to bomb an American airliner departing from Frankfurt Airport. It certainly was possible that Pan Am 103 had been blown up because of the *Vincennes* incident. That possibility, however, brought investigators no closer to knowing who, among countless numbers of terrorists, was responsible for the bombing of Flight 103.

So the detectives persisted, interviewing anyone remotely connected to the case. Before long, they had learned details that helped them narrow the field of suspects dramatically.

The pattern of destruction clearly indicated that the force of the blast had been near the front of the airplane. By meticulously reconstructing the fragmented pieces of the plane, investigators were able to learn that the bomb had been placed in a luggage container in the forward cargo hold. By terrible luck, it exploded exactly where it could do the most damage—at station 41, which housed the electrical system that powered the entire airplane. That explained why Captain MacQuarrie had no time to respond with a distress signal. The reconstruction provided even more vital information: The suitcase that contained the bomb exploded in 14L, the cargo hold carrying bags from Frankfurt. The suitcase must have been loaded on the plane at the Frankfurt Airport.

If that discovery did not particularly indicate that Ahmed Jibril's PFLP-GC group was involved, the

The inside of a Toshiba radio cassette recorder carries a bomb and trigger. German police distributed this photo to international airlines soon after the Lockerbie crash.

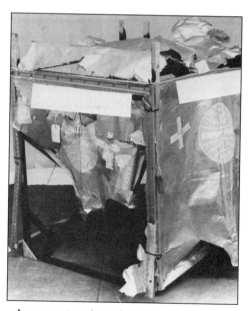

A reconstruction of the Pan Am cargo container shows the effects of the explosion.

next finding certainly seemed to. Detectives were able to piece together enough fragments from the explosive device to learn that it had been contained in a Toshiba cassette recorder. It was not the same model as the one confiscated in the West German raids two months prior to the crash—that one had one speaker, this one had two—but that was a minor detail. The PFLP-GC had emerged as the prime suspect in the Lockerbie bombing.

Other suspects were not automatically ruled out, though. In the months following the tragedy, investigators pieced together a number of theories regarding the case. Some suggested that the CIA was involved in some way. Four CIA agents were among the victims of the crash, and rumors emerged about a briefcase containing secret documents. Had one of the agents been the target of some plot? Another proposed theory was that the U.S. Drug Enforcement Administration (DEA) was running an operation to catch drug smugglers that backfired horribly. The DEA had an agreement with airport personnel to let an unchecked drug-laden bag get through security, but a terrorist who knew of the plan switched the bag with one containing the bomb. Because of the agreement with security, the bomb went undetected.

While those theories were quickly disproved, the theory that the PFLP-GC was behind the bombing went virtually unchallenged for nearly two years. Then in the summer of 1991, startling new evidence overturned just about everything investigators thought they knew.

New Clues Changed Case

The key breakthrough in the case hinged on a microchip found in the wreckage of Flight 103. Forensic experts learned that the chip—a tiny triggering device for detonating a bomb—did not match the detonators in the bombs confiscated from the PFLP-GC. The Palestinian group's detonators were wired to altimeter devices set to go off when the plane reached a preset altitude. But the detonator fragment from the crash site was attached to an ordinary timer that had been set for a certain hour. Also, the PFLP-GC detonators were made in Czechoslovakia. The detonator found in the wreckage was Swiss-made. These clues seemed to suggest the involvement of a different terrorist group.

A young CIA analyst began to wonder if someone other than the PFLP-GC might be involved in the Pan Am bombing. Working on a hunch, he looked for a "fingerprint" that might link the Pan Am bombing to earlier incidents in the CIA's files. (Fingerprints are what forensic experts call the telltale characteristics of exploding devices). The analyst connected the Pan Am bombing to three earlier bombing incidents in Africa, all carried out by Libya. One of the cases involved the arrest of two men at Dakar Airport in Senegal in February 1988. The men were carrying twenty pounds of Semtex and TNT explosives and triggering devices identical to the microchip fragment found at Lockerbie. The two men—Mohammed Naydi and Mansour Omran Saber—were Libyan intelli-

Did Libyan leader Moammar Kadaffi mastermind the Lockerbie crash?

gence agents. They were never formally charged, and Senegal released them in June 1988.

Lockerbie investigators now suspect that the two men may have been involved in the Pan Am case, and that Libyan officials were behind both the Senegal incident and the Flight 103 bombing. With this new evidence, the motive for the Pan Am bombing is thought to be revenge for the U.S. bombing of Libya's capital, Tripoli, in 1986. The U.S. attack, which was believed to have killed forty people including Libyan leader Moammar Kadaffi's daughter, was carried out in retaliation for an earlier Libyan-inspired bombing in Germany.

Based on this new evidence, investigators believe that officials in the Libyan government held a meeting in September 1988 at Libyan intelligence headquarters, and planned several attacks against the United States and France. The destruction of Pan Am Flight 103 was one of the attacks planned at this meeting. The French government, leading its own investigation, believes officials at that meeting also ordered the bombing of a French airplane (UTA Flight 772, which blew up in September 1989, killing 171 people). The attack on France, according to authorities, was intended as revenge for French aid to Chad, a country which defeated Libya in a conflict over territory.

Libya's foreign minister has denied that his government was involved in either the bombing of Flight 103

A team of American investigators inspects the debris of UTA Flight 772 in the Tenere Desert of Niger. Authorities believe Libya ordered the bombing of the airplane as revenge for French aid to Chad.

or the French airliner, calling the allegations "prejudiced and silly." Nonetheless, the director of the French investigation is reportedly close to issuing charges against top Libyan officials who were at the 1988 meeting, and U.S. Justice Department officials are preparing a case of their own.

Even though the Lockerbie investigators are encouraged by the breakthrough in the case, they know they still lack important information about the bombing. They do not know exactly how the bomb got on the plane, for example, or who put it there. They are no longer sure which terrorist group was involved, or if there are links to other groups or governments of which they might be unaware. Such details will be necessary to make a convincing case in a courtroom.

So the investigators press on, determined to uncover the facts they need to bring the perpetrators to justice. The investigation team itself is rather remarkable. Truly an international effort, it has required the cooperation of several countries and numerous agencies and intelligence networks. By August of 1989, the Lockerbie team had traveled to nearly forty countries, collecting evidence and chasing down clues. It is not very often that police officers and secret agents work side by side, as they have for over two years now in the Lockerbie case.

Because the disaster took place on Scottish soil, the Scottish have led the investigation. When the case does go to trial, it will be heard there, if all the countries involved agree. As lord advocate of Scotland, Peter Fraser is responsible for prosecuting the case. He waits, often impatiently, for the evidence he needs to bring the case to court one day. But he would rather wait, years if that is what it takes, than risk losing an opportunity to right the terrible wrong committed over Lockerbie.

Five

Ending the Cycle of Violence

On a gray, drizzly afternoon two weeks after the crash of Flight 103, a great crowd filled Lockerbie's Dryfesdale Parish Church. It was January 3, 1989. The occasion was a memorial service to honor those who had died in the disaster, and people spilled out onto the steps of the church and into the adjoining graveyard. Prime Minister Margaret Thatcher sat in a front pew. British transport secretary Paul Channing and U.S. ambassador to Great Britain Charles Price II were among the government officials present. Television cameras carried the ceremony to homes across Scotland and northern England.

For forty minutes or more, the town of Lockerbie came to a standstill, united in a public demonstration of grief. Even the local police station stopped work to watch the service on a television screen. The congregation read psalms, sang hymns, and listened to several clergymen speak words of consolation. The Right Reverend Professor James Whyte, moderator of the General Assembly of the Church of Scotland, gave the main address, speaking in a voice moved with emotion. "It is not only pain and grief we feel at this catastrophe," he said, "it is also indignation. For this was not an unforeseeable natural disaster, such as an earthquake. Nor was it the result of human error or carelessness. This, we now know, was an act of human wickedness. That such carnage of the young and of the innocent should have been willed by men in cold and calculated evil is horror upon horror."

The news that a terrorist's bomb had caused the downing of Flight 103 shocked and angered everyone. For the family and friends of crash victims, it meant facing the fact that their loved ones had been murdered. This knowledge somehow made the tragedy harder to bear. Many would have been consoled to think that the people important to them simply had been victims of misfortune.

The Desire for Revenge

In his stirring sermon, Whyte cautioned against the desire for revenge. He said that some in the media were calling for retaliation and urging the United States to use military power against the terrorists. That, the reverend warned, would

All over the world, people gathered to mourn the passengers of Flight 103. Here, friends and family honor a Syracuse University student in Wyckoff, New Jersey.

only continue the endless cycle of violence. He advised others to concentrate on the good that had come of the tragedy. People had shown courage and compassion to one another, and a wonderful community had sprung up ready to reach out to those in need.

It was in this spirit that family members of crash victims met just weeks after the disaster to form a group called Victims of Pan Am Flight 103. The group was formed on February 19, 1989, by Bert Ammerman, a school superintendent from New Jersey who had lost his thirty-six-year-old brother, Tom, in the crash. These survivors wanted to work to ensure that a tragedy like the bombing of Pan Am 103 would never happen again. They wanted to find out why the bombing oc-curred, and what needed to be changed to prevent future attacks. If they could spare others the grief and pain they felt, some good would come of this tragic event.

Victims of Pan Am Flight 103

The more than three hundred members formed four committees—political, press, investigative, and legal. By summer 1989, Victims of Pan Am Flight 103 was publishing its own newsletter, picketing Pan Am's office building in New York City, and meeting with a number of U.S. senators. The group was also in contact with a similar group that had been formed in Great Britain, the United Kingdom Families of Flight 103.

Both groups are still actively working to achieve several goals:

Rows of coffins of the victims of the crash fill the town hall in Lockerbie.

the adoption of more sophisticated equipment for detecting explosives and weapons; higher security standards and better-trained security staff at airports; the notification of passengers and airline personnel when there is a serious security risk; and better communication among government agencies responsible for investigating terrorist activity.

In addition, the Victims of Pan Am 103 lobbied the government for an independent investigation into the cause of the disaster. Because of the families' persistent efforts, the president's office appointed a special seven-member committee. Its task was to try to answer every question raised by the victims' families and to suggest ways to prevent future terrorist attacks.

Inadequate Airline Security

In May 1990, the President's Commission on Aviation Security and Terrorism published the results of its seven-month study. The committee found that "the destruction of Flight 103 may well have been preventable." They concluded that, although other factors were involved, the disaster was able to occur largely because of inadequate airline security. Investigators do not yet know exactly how the bomb got onto the plane, so they cannot point with certainty to any one security failure. But they do know that the bomb was inside a piece of luggage checked onto Flight 103. Obviously, there were problems with the screening of baggage and passengers.

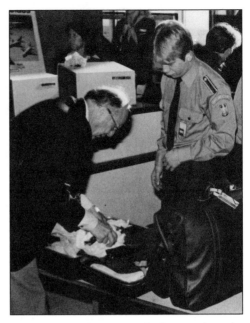

A bomb can be smuggled on a plane in a number of ways, especially in interline baggage.

A bomb can be smuggled onto a plane in only a handful of ways. An unsuspecting passenger might be tricked into carrying it aboard as a favor (for example, a terrorist asks the passenger to bring a present to an American friend). A self-sacrificing terrorist might board the plane with a bomb in his own suitcase; needless to say, this does not happen frequently. More often, a bag containing the bomb is slipped in with the bags of passengers. To prevent this last method, airlines must keep track of which bags belong to which passengers.

Interline, or transfer, baggage—luggage transferred from one airplane to another for a connecting flight—poses a special security risk. It is easier to lose track of, espe-

NEW TECHNOLOGIES FOR AIRPORT SECURITY

Conventional airport security devices such as the X-ray machine and the magnetometer are ineffective when it comes to detecting the increasingly sophisticated methods used by many terrorists. Scientists are researching new technologies, however, and several detection devices currently under development look promising.

Vapor detectors sniff the vapors or particles that leak from a bag containing explosives or measure the physical or chemical content of a piece of luggage without opening it. These devices try, for example, to detect the nitrogen present in organic explosives such as Semtex, the plastic explosive used in the Pan Am Flight 103 bombing. Though promising, this technology needs further development and testing.

A device that detects explosives by picking up the lead and mercury used in detonators is currently being researched. So is "backscatter" X-ray equipment, reputed to be more effective than the X-ray machines now in use. One airline currently tests for baro-metric bombs, similar to the one used on Flight 103, by putting all cargo into an atmospheric-pressure chamber, where it is "flown" at the plane's highest altitude, and "landed" as many times as the plane will be landed.

The President's Commission was highly critical of another type of technology, thermal neutron analysis technology or TNA. The FAA wants to require airlines to buy TNA. A TNA machine uses small amounts of nuclear radiation to detect the physical and chemical properties of cargo and luggage. According to the commission, the lowest amount of Semtex the TNA machine is capable of detecting is still twice the amount believed to have been used to destroy Flight 103. The commission strongly recommends that the FAA not require use of TNA equipment until it is developed further. In the meantime, advises the commission, the FAA should remain committed to the research and development of explosive-detection systems.

This worker operates a Thermal Neutron Analysis machine to detect explosives like Semtex.

cially at an airport as busy as Frankfurt's, where there are many connecting flights. For example, sometimes a passenger misses a connecting flight, but his or her bags are on board. In such cases, airline officials should be suspicious. What if the passenger deliberately missed the flight because there was a bomb in his or her suitcase, intended for the next leg of the journey?

Pan Am Violated Rules

In fall 1988, a time of heightened tension over increased terrorism, the FAA had strict guidelines on what was to be done in such situations. The FAA did not consistently enforce the rules, however, and Pan Am did not adhere to them. In fact, Pan Am's handling of interline baggage at the time of the Flight 103 tragedy almost ensured a disaster. FAA regulations clearly stated that any checked bag that could not be matched to someone who had boarded a flight must be opened and physically searched. Any luggage belonging to someone who failed to appear for a flight had to be taken off the plane and searched. These procedures could be time-consuming, though, and sometimes threatened to delay flights at the busy Frankfurt Airport. Several months before the crash of Flight 103, Pan Am decided to X-ray interline baggage. In clear violation of FAA rules, Pan Am stopped hand-searching unaccompanied bags or trying to match them to passengers.

Pan Am employees working at Frankfurt Main on December 21, the day of the crash, had not been told about either the Helsinki warning or the Toshiba cassette-player bomb confiscated just two months earlier. The X-ray operator screening interline baggage had been on the job for a month and a half and had received only half a day of training. As baggage handlers gathered the interline luggage destined for the first leg of Flight 103's trip, they made no attempt to match the bags to the interline passengers boarding the flight. Nor were any of the bags physically searched. They were X-rayed as they descended the loading ramp, but the Toshiba cassette-player bomb—which detectives believe was in one of the suitcases loaded at Frankfurt—was designed to elude X-ray detection. When Flight 103 left for London, Pan Am security workers had no way of knowing if an extra bag, unattached to any passenger, was on board.

Passengers Not Questioned

Nor did Pan Am know as much about the passengers as they should have. FAA regulations required security employees to question interline passengers to determine if they fit the profile of someone likely to carry explosives aboard a plane. This policy was meant to pinpoint people who were deliberately concealing bombs as well as those who had been fooled into carrying one by someone else. Passengers who fit the profile were to be singled out for further screening. But several

Lax security measures for interline baggage at Frankfurt International Airport may have led to the crash of Flight 103.

interline passengers boarding Flight 103 at Frankfurt on December 21 were never questioned. Several more identified as needing further screening did not receive it.

Pan Am employees at London's Heathrow Airport who gathered interline baggage for the London, New York leg of Flight 103 also disregarded FAA regulations. As in Frankfurt, these bags were neither physically searched nor matched with the number of interline passengers on the plane. The baggage was X-rayed and loaded into a container outside Pan Am's offices to await the arrival of Flight 103 from Frankfurt. The partially loaded baggage container was then left unattended, curtain open, for over half an hour. At the time, this was not a violation of FAA regulations.

When the first leg of Flight 103 landed at Heathrow, luggage was taken directly from it and put into the unguarded baggage container. It was not X-rayed or screened again. Pan Am relied instead on the screening that had been done at Frankfurt. The filled container was then put into the hold of the 747, just hours before it would blow up in the night sky over Lockerbie.

Major Security Flaws

Someone who wanted to slip a suitcase with a bomb in it would have had plenty of opportunities. Even more alarming was the President's Commission finding that the security violations that enabled the bombing to occur were still uncorrected nine months after the tragedy. FAA investigations following the disaster revealed that Pan Am's security problems at Frankfurt persisted. A regular inspection in May 1989 uncovered major security flaws, including failure to track passengers adequately, failure to guard aircraft, and failure to search maintenance workers. An unannounced FAA inspection in August 1989 found many of the same problems still unremedied. Planes continued to be left unguarded, and personnel with access to the aircraft were not being searched.

By mid-September, after repeated warnings and much pressure, Pan Am finally corrected its security problems. It took only one week with the concentrated attention of management to change the situation. Pan Am was able to pass routine inspections again, and the FAA called Frankfurt a "model station." For security violations at Frankfurt and Heathrow, both during and after Flight 103, however, the FAA fined Pan Am $630,000.

The FAA Found Guilty

The President's Commission also criticized the FAA. In fact, one of the major conclusions of the commission was that the aviation security system in general was flawed and in need of major reform. The commission concluded that the FAA only reacts to tragedies, failing to anticipate and plan for future threats. The commission also learned that, prior to the Lockerbie crash, the FAA failed to enforce its own policies. As early as April 1988, Pan Am was no longer following the FAA's written procedure calling for the matching of interline baggage with passengers. The FAA learned this in October 1988 when it inspected Pan Am's Frankfurt operation, yet it did not fine Pan Am.

Since the downing of Flight 103, the FAA has instituted stricter security guidelines. If these had been in place earlier, they may have helped to prevent the Lockerbie tragedy. Fourteen days after the disaster, the FAA proposed a regulation that baggage containers must be sealed and under surveillance at all times. Another new policy required that every suitcase loaded onto an international flight must belong to a passenger who is also on that flight. Unaccompanied bags, whether searched or not, can no longer be stowed.

Pan Am, too, has made some security changes. It extended the training time for its Alert security program from three hours to eight days. It also bought new equipment, including a color X-ray monitor to replace one that had been broken for several months.

In addition to its specific recommendations for the FAA and Pan Am, the President's Commission report contains more than sixty specific recommendations for improving aviation security and preventing future terrorist attacks. The commission strongly recommends that the U.S. government pursue and punish terrorists, even using military force against them. Another suggestion is that victims of terrorist acts directed against the U.S. gov-

United States Senator Frank R. Lautenberg, a former member of the President's Commission. He and the other members of the commission placed much of the blame for the crash on the FAA.

ernment should receive special financial compensation.

Although neither of these recommendations have been implemented, a handful of others have. An antiterrorism bill, which grew out of the commission's recommendations, was signed into law November 16, 1990. The law authorizes up to $7 million be spent in 1991 to upgrade security at airlines and airports. The bill creates a new position to lobby for security issues at the U.S. Department of Transportation. It also requires the FAA to develop guidelines for notifying the public of bomb threats. According to Transportation Secretary Samuel Skinner, the law is "a significant milestone for . . . the families

Police officers armed with weapons patrol London's Heathrow Airport in an effort to deter terrorists. Stringent antiterrorist measures have been recommended for other airports.

of the victims of the Pan Am 103 tragedy . . . and everyone who flies."

In another step, the U.S. government increased its reward fund to $4 million for information on terrorists. Television and radio commercials produced in six languages ask, "Are you the next hero?" and encourage citizens to provide information concerning terrorists to collect cash rewards. In announcing the program, a government official explained that there are "ways that governments and citizens can work together to ensure that the warped psychology of the terrorist does not dominate our lives or distort our policies."

Making Security Systems Work

Many experts argue that developing equipment that can detect small amounts of explosives should be a top priority for aviation security. The bomb that blew up Pan Am 103 was cleverly hidden, and, according to an explosives expert who testified before a Scottish inquiry into the bombing, the Toshiba tape player containing the bomb would not have looked suspicious from the outside. If it had been turned on—security personnel routinely ask passengers to switch on cassette players—it would have worked like an ordinary machine. The expert testified further that it would take an unusually experienced operator to spot the device on an X-ray machine.

The latest laws and most sophisticated technology amount to nothing, however, unless the people behind the machines are motivated to making the system work. One of the lessons of Lockerbie is that aviation security has to become a matter of utmost priority. Hiring committed, qualified employees and providing them with extensive training is a must. The events leading up to the fall of Flight 103, in which hairdressers became baggage screeners and security seemed more about show than substance, cannot be repeated.

No Standard System in Effect

Although U.S. carriers at foreign airports have done much to improve security, there is still no standard system for international air security in effect. Since the Lockerbie bombing, two more international flights have been the target of terrorist bombs. A French flight from Brazzaville, the Congo, to Paris was destroyed in September 1989, killing 171 people. Two months later, 107 people were killed when Avianca Flight 203 from Bogota to Cali, Colombia, was destroyed. Unless international standards can be greatly improved, airplanes will continue to be potential terrorist targets.

Even if the threat of terrorist attack cannot be completely eliminated, everything must be done to keep it as small as possible. The Lockerbie investigation team is dedicated to finding those responsible for the bombing and bringing them to justice. They want to send terrorists the message that their actions will not be tolerated. William Ses-

sions, the director of the FBI, announced in November 1990 that the investigation may take years, but he is confident the bombers will be brought before a court. "We will not let go," he promised. "We are not only tenacious, but we are diligent about our responsibility."

There are others, too, who will not let go. To their credit, the Victims of Pan Am Flight 103 do what they can to keep the issue in the public eye. Exactly 103 days after the bombing, they led a vigil outside the White House. Afterward, Bert Ammerman and three other group members met with President George Bush, who again pledged his commitment to finding the terrorists. On December 21, 1990, the second anniversary of the disaster, victims' families gathered outside the Pan Am building in New York City to read the names of those who died in the crash.

Reforms Not Through Yet

The reforms now in place have largely been brought about by the efforts and dedication of Victims of Pan Am 103. But they are not through yet. Until international air security is vastly improved and the terrorists face trial, those whose lives were forever changed by the events at Lockerbie on December 21, 1988, will not give up. Thanks to them, countless others may already have been spared the suffering and grief of another disaster like the downing of Flight 103.

Epilogue
Finding the Missing Pieces

Unlike the sinking of the *Titanic* or the explosion of the space shuttle *Challenger*, the destruction of Pan Am Flight 103 was deliberate. A handful of people meant for it to happen: They planned the act and planted the deadly bomb. As the investigation into Lockerbie showed, carelessness on the part of many people made it easier for the terrorists to achieve their murderous ends. If it were not for the security oversights, the tragedy might not have happened. But the knowledge that the Lockerbie crash had been intended and premeditated adds a terrible dimension to the disaster.

In late March 1991, the results of a Scottish study of the safety issues related to Lockerbie were released. The report, which blamed Pan Am for the bombing, confirmed the findings of the President's Commission. It revealed that the suitcase containing the bomb could not be traced to any passenger on Flight 103 (from either the Frankfurt or London connections) and Pan Am had no system in place to discover this. If Pan Am had been tracking interline baggage, security employees would have found and searched the extra bag. According to the report, "such a precaution might have avoided the deaths."

The bombing of Flight 103 was one of the worst acts of terror ever directed against the United States—a bombing that took 270 lives, 192 of them American. It led to the largest international criminal inquiry in history. Thanks to recent findings, the Lockerbie investigation appears to be nearing a close. Its success stems from the skill and dedication of hard-working detectives, of course, but as with any investigation, sheer luck has played a part too. As one official pointed out, if the bomb had exploded ten or fifteen minutes later, the plane would have been over the Atlantic Ocean and investigators would have retrieved nothing.

George Esson, director of the Scottish investigation, described the ongoing effort in these words: "What we are doing, in effect, is trying to piece together an international terrorist jigsaw. We have some of the pieces. Some we are trying to place. And some we are trying to find." Detectives and intelligence experts are finally on the brink of assembling the jigsaw.

The Garden of Remembrance in Dryfesdal Cemetery, outside Lockerbie. Plaques in the garden bear the names of all 270 victims of the incident.

Glossary

BKA: *Bundeskriminalamt;* the West German federal police force.

counterterrorism: Terrorism in reaction to or retaliation for another act of terrorism.

decompression: A reduction in atmospheric pressure.

extremist: A supporter of extreme doctrines or practices, especially in relation to political or religious beliefs.

fuselage: The body of an airplane, to which the wing and tail surfaces are attached.

forensic specialist: One who uses scientific and investigative techniques to learn about criminal activity.

interline: The transfer of passengers, baggage, or cargo from one air carrier to another during travel.

PFLP-GC: Popular Front for the Liberation of Palestine—General Command; the Palestinian terrorist group lead by Ahmed Jibril.

Richter scale: A scale ranging from 1 to 10 used to measure the intensity of an earthquake (named after Charles Richter, a seismologist).

seismograph: An instrument that measures and records the vibrations of an earthquake.

Semtex: A plastic explosive manufactured in Czechoslovakia and used to make bombs that are difficult to detect with conventional airport security machines.

tarmac: A road, airport runway, or parking lot paved with a layer of tarmacadam, a paving material consisting of coarse crushed stone mixed with tar.

terrorism: The use of threats and violence to force and intimidate others, especially for political purposes.

transponder: A radar transceiver that automatically transmits a signal when it receives designated incoming signals; sends flight information to air traffic control.

Suggestions for Further Reading

Bremner, Charles, Richard Evans, and Douglas Broom, "Anguished Vigil at Two Airports," *The London Times,* December 22, 1988.

Elliott, Harvey, "The Crash of Flight PA 103," *The London Times,* December 22, 1988.

Emerson, Steven, and Brian Duffy, *The Fall of Pan Am 103: Inside the Lockerbie Investigation.* New York: G.P. Putnam's Sons, 1990.

Evans, Michael, Thomas Prentice, and Michael Binyon. "Embassy Bulletin Told of Terror Plot," *The London Times,* December 23, 1988.

Gill, Kerry, "Visiting Thatcher Extends Sympathy," *The London Times,* December 23, 1988.

Greaves, William, "Solving the Jigsaw of Tragedy," *The London Times,* December 23, 1988.

Johnston, David, *Lockerbie: The Tragedy of Flight 103.* New York: St. Martin's Press, 1989.

McFadden, Robert D., "Vigils, Tears and Grief for Victims of Disaster," *The New York Times,* December 23, 1988.

Office of the President, *President's Commission on Aviation Security and Terrorism.* Washington, DC: Government Printing Office, 1990.

Rule, Sheila, "In Scottish Village, Numbed Disbelief," *The New York Times,* December 23, 1988.

Index

About the Author

The author, Madelyn Horton is a student in the Ph.D. program in English at the University of Washington. She lives in Seattle with her husband and son. *The Lockerbie Airline Crash* is her first book for Lucent Books.

Picture Credits

Cover Illustration: Brian McGovern, McGovern Graphics
AP/Wide World Photos, 9, 11, 13 (all), 17, 19, 20, 25, 27, 28, 30, 38, 41, 44 (top), 45, 46, 49, 51, 52, 54, 56, 59
Gamma Liaison, 16 (right), 22
Lockerbie Academy, 39
Office of Frank R. Lautenberg, 55
The Press Association Ltd., 29, 31, 32, 34, 35, 37, 42, 44 (bottom), 50
Reuters/Bettmann, 15, 40
UPI/Bettmann Newsphotos, 16 (left), 18